100
SILLY
DINOSAUR
JOKES
FOR KIDS

Jess Kiddin

ULYSSES BOOKS
FOR YOUNG READERS

Published by:
Ulysses Books for Young Readers
an imprint of Ulysses Press
PO Box 3440
Berkeley, CA 94703

ISBN: 978-1-64604-690-4
Library of Congress Control Number: 2024931469

Printed in the United States
2 4 6 8 10 9 7 5 3 1

Image credits: *cover*—green dinosaur © Sararoom
Design/shutterstock.com, blue dinosaur © braingraph/
shutterstock.com; *interior*—bottom border © Studio
Ayutaka/shutterstock.com, top border and title page ©
BudOlga/shutterstock.com, T. rex cartoon created with
the assistance of DALL-E.

Why was the T. rex upset?

Because he was happy and he knew it...

Why did the dinosaur cross the road?

Because the chicken hadn't evolved yet.

What do you get when a T. rex meets a human?

Just a T. rex.

What kind of dinosaurs used to burst suddenly?

Tricera-pops!

What did the dinosaur use to cut wood?

A dino-saw.

What was the name of the fastest dinosaur?

PRONTOsaurus!

What weighs 800 pounds and sticks to the roof of your mouth?

A peanut butter and Stegosaurus sandwich.

What do you call a dinosaur wizard?

A dinosorcerer.

How did the dinosaur feel after its nap?

Jurras-tic!

What happened after the dinosaur took the school bus home?

It had to bring it back.

Why was the Stegosaurus such a good volleyball player?

He could really spike the ball!

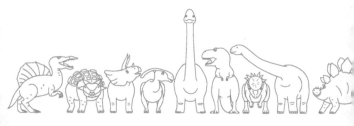

**What do you call
someone who puts
their right hand in the
mouth of a T. rex?**

Lefty.

Why did the dinosaur go to the doctor?

Because it had a dino-SORE.

What does a dinosaur call a porcupine?

A toothbrush.

What do you call a group of dinosaurs who sing?

A Tyranno-chorus.

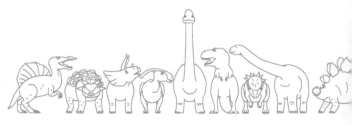

What do you call a paleontologist who sleeps all the time?

Lazy bones.

Knock, knock.
Who's there?
Dino.
Dino who?

I dino, I'm too scared
to open the door.

Why do museums exhibit old dinosaur bones?

They can't afford the new ones.

What kind of dinosaurs make good police officers?

Tricera-cops.

What did the dinosaur call her shirt store?

Try Sarah's Tops.

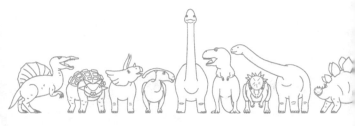

What do you call a dinosaur wearing a cowboy hat and boots?

Tyrannosaurus tex!

What did the caveman say as he slid down the dinosaur's neck?

"So long!"

What do you get when you cross a pig and a dinosaur?

Jurassic pork.

What kind of materials do dinosaurs use for the floor of their homes?

Rep-tiles.

Why can't you hear a Pterodactyl when it goes to the bathroom?

The pee is silent.

**What do you get
when a dinosaur
walks through the
berry patch?**

Jam.

**Why did the
Apatosaurus devour
the factory?**

Because she was
a plant-eater.

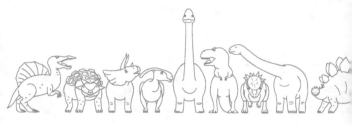

Why did the Archaeopteryx catch the worm?

Because it was an early bird!

What's the best thing to do if you see a Tyrannosaurus rex?

Hope he doesn't see you too.

What do you call a dinosaur that asks a lot of deep questions?

A Philosiraptor.

Which reindeer is the dinosaurs' least favorite?

Comet.

Why did carnivorous dinosaurs eat raw meat?

They didn't know how to BBQ!

How do you invite a dinosaur to a cafe?

Tea, Rex?

Why should you never ask a dinosaur to read you a story?

Their tales are too long.

When can three giant dinosaurs get under an umbrella and not get wet?

When it's not raining.

What game do pet Brontosauruses like to play with humans?

Squash.

Why can't a Tyrannosaurus rex do push-ups?

Because they're extinct.

Which dinosaur can jump higher than a house?

Trick question! All dinosaurs—houses can't jump.

How do Tyrannosaurus rexes settle arguments?

A quick game of scissors, scissors, scissors.

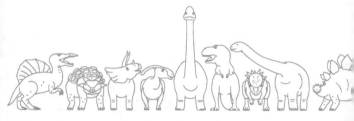

How do you know
that a Seismosaurus
is under your bed?

**Because your nose
is only two inches
from the ceiling.**

What's as big as a dinosaur but weighs nothing?

Dinosaur shadows.

What was T. rex's favorite number?

Eight (ate)!

What would happen if a 100-ton Brachiosaurus stepped on you?

You'd be deeply impressed.

What did the T. rex say at lunchtime?

Wanna grab a bite!

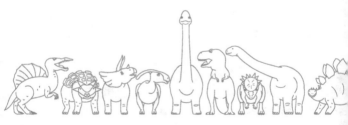

Which dinosaur LOVES Christmas?

Tree rex.

Do you think anything could tricera-top these dinosaur puns?

I dino what to tell you, but probably not.

What should you do when a dinosaur sneezes?

Get out of the way!

How do you know if there is a dinosaur in your fridge?

The door won't shut!

What do you call a dinosaur with one eye?

An eye-saur!

How did the cavemen survive dinosaur attacks?

They stayed 56 million years away.

What did the dinosaur say to the cashier?

"Keep the climate change."

What do you call a short spiky dinosaur that's fallen down the stairs?

Ankle-is-sore-us.

Do you know how long dinosaurs lived?

Very similar to the short ones.

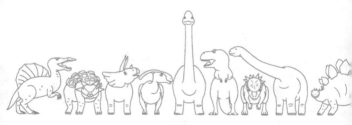

How did the dinosaur feel after it ate a pillow?

Down in the mouth.

What do you call a dinosaur that won't stop talking?

A dino-bore!

Why didn't the dinosaur cross the road?

Because roads didn't exist!

**Knock, knock.
Who's there?
Dinosaurp.
Dinosaurp who?**

**Haha, you said
"dinosaur poo."**

What kind of dinosaur can you ride in a rodeo?

A Bronco-saurus!

What do you call a deaf dinosaur?

Anything you like— it can't hear you!

What did the dinosaur put on her burger?

Dinosauce.

What do you call a near-sighted dinosaur?

A Do-you-think-he-saurus rex.

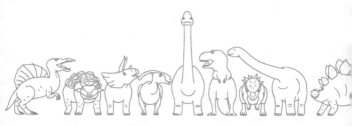

What do you call a dinosaur fart?

Exstinktion!

What's worse than a giraffe with a sore throat?

A Diplodocus with a sore throat.

What do dinosaurs use to dig tunnels?

DINOmite!

What should you use to fight a T. rex?

A dino-sword.

What do you call a polite dinosaur?

A Pleaseyosaur.

What should you do if you find a dinosaur in your bed?

Find somewhere else to sleep!

Why does a Brontosaurus have a long neck?

Its feet smell really bad.

What do you call a dinosaur who is a noisy sleeper?

Tyranno-snorus rex.

What do you call a dinosaur ghost?

A Scaredactyl.

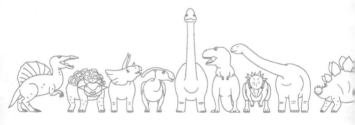

Why was the dinosaur nervous about the future?

He knew he was just a big chicken.

What's a dinosaur's favorite quote?

"Jurassic times call for Jurassic measures!"

What comes after extinction?

Y-stinction.

What do you call anxious dinos?

Nervous rex.

What vehicle does a Tyrannosaurus rex use to travel from planet to planet?

A dino-saucer.

What do you call a T. rex who hates losing?

A saur loser.

Knock, knock.
Who's there?
Terry.
Terry who?

Terry Dactyl!

What came after
the dinosaur?

Its tail.

How does a dinosaur apologize?

I'm-so-saurus.

What do you call a dinosaur that left its armor out in the rain?

A Stegosau-rust.

Where do dinosaurs spend their pocket money?

Dino stores.

What do you call a dinosaur that never gives up?

Try-try-try-ceratops!

What do you call it when a dinosaur gets a goal?

A dino-score!

**Knock, knock.
Who's there?
Dinosaur.
Dinosaur who?**

**Dinosaurs don't say
"who," they roar.**

What is in the middle of dinosaurs?

The letter S.

What did dinosaurs use to drive their cars?

Fossil fuels.

**Which dinosaur
has 3 horns and is
seen on 4 wheels?**

**A Triceratops on
a skateboard.**

Why couldn't the dinosaur use its computer?

It ate the mouse.

What's the best way to talk to a Velociraptor?

Really long distance.

What do you call a baby dinosaur?

A Wee-rex!

What do you call a dinosaur with a rich vocabulary?

A thesaurus.

What do you call twin dinosaurs?

Pair-odactyls!

What's the best way to raise a baby Brachiosaurus?

With a crane.

What's a child's favorite dinosaur?

A Toys-"R"-Us.

What does a Triceratops sit on?

Its Tricera-bottom.

What do you call dinosaur car accidents?

Tyrannosaurus wrecks.

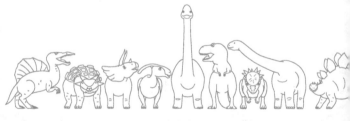

What do you call a dinosaur that doesn't take a bath?

Stink-o-saurus rex.

**Knock, knock.
Who's there?
Annie.
Annie who?**

**Annie dinosaur can
swallow you whole.**

What makes more noise than a dinosaur?

Two dinosaurs.

Knock, knock.
Who's there?
Tye.
Tye who?

Tyrannosaurus
wrecks this house.

Knock, knock.
Who's there?
Haven.
Haven who?

**Haven you heard enough
dinosaur jokes by now?**

Add Your Own Jokes!

_____

_____

_____

_____

_____

_____

_____

_____

_____

_____

_____

_____

_____